a.b.s. clothing · abraham · abrams · achenbaum · ackerman · adelphi university · adoni · adp · advantage title · aetna · ag mastercraft · ahnalt · aip · alert fire company · allen dental medical development · allen labs · allstate · alteka corporation · amati · ameribuild · americana corporate center · amzallag · andrea electronics · andrew auto dealership · andrew hotel · apollo · arkwin · armon · armonas · ashner · athletes foot · aviram · ayre · aziz · bahar · baharestani · bank of smithtown · barami · baranello · barclay · barley ziecheck offices · barrocas · barrons publishing · bass · bassuk · baum · beck · beckman · beer · beige · bell · bellerose fire house · belvedere offices · benalloul · benenson · bennett · berkley · berlin · berman · bernard · besen · bied · bikoff building · blau · blue rock development · blumencrantz · blumenfeld · blumenthal · boca rio golf club · boces · body design by gilda · boilermakers local 5 · boisi · borek · botanical design · boyar · brae burn country club · braverman · brensilver · breslin · brock · brodsky · brooks · brostoff · brudner · bryant & cooper · bufkin · buscemi · byron · c.w. post · cablevision · calcasola · calverton · camera company · canon · careers · carillo · carlyle hotel · cayne · certilman · cga computers · charno · chartash · chasanoff · chemical bank · cheyenne softwarev · child · choi · ciliberti offices · cineplex odean · clappers · clifford · cline davis mann · coda · cohen · cohn · colarossi · cold spring country club · coleman · colin management · columbia management · com center · community national bank · complements · complink · conference of american rabbis · continanza · convent of the sisters of mercy · cooper · cooperman · coppola-pine salon · corporate national realty · cosulich · court square · crest hollow country club · crispi · cross country paper products · crossways park · curto · cushman & wakefield · cut & curl · cutco industries · cvs · d'addario · dante · davidson · davis · deanto · deepdale golf club · del labs · delco development · deli king · delmonte · dent · deutsch · diamond · diebold · difazio · diresta · dns metal · doff · dolgi · dombeck · donaldson · dorman · dubner · dubofsky · earth health · efrem · egremont inn · eisen · eldon realty · ellstein · elmhurst dairies · engineers country club · entel · equinox · errico · esrail · essex manufacturing · estee lauder · etra · ettinger · evans development · executive life · fabricant · farber · farkas · feinsod · feldberg · feldman · feldstein · fells · feng chung offices · fern · ferrari restaurant · feuerman · fine · finger · fiore · fischer · fishman · flanzig · flax · fleres · floral park school · fluke manufacturing · forman · fortunoff · foster · founders room · four queens ice cream · frank · frankel · fresh meadows country club · fried · friedman · friends academy · fromer · fuld · g-4 development · gambrell · gans · ganz · garden school · gauze & effect · gelber · genicoff · gerla · giffords · gilardian · giles & lewis · gindi · giordano · giraldi · gitto · giuseppe · glachman · glen head country club · glick · goebel · gold · goldberg · goldberger · goldman · goldsmith · golf etc. · good · goodman · goodstein · gordon · gottlieb · gramercy park medical · grand island · great expectations · great neck art center · great neck pediatric · great neck plaza · great neck properties · greenberg · greenblatt industries · greenbriar mall · greenfield · greenwald · greystone · grocery haulers · groden · gross · grossberg · grumman · gsa · gucker · gutman · gutterman · hammerman jewelry · hampshire country club · handley · harbor hills country club · harbor plaza · harbor view athletic club · harrison · hart · hastings tile · hauppauge office park · hayim · hearst magazines · heilbron · helene · heller · herman · hewlett packard · hineni center · hirschhorn · hitzig · hoffman · hollander offices · hommel construction · honeywell farms · honigman · hoops · horn · horowitz · howell · huntington crescent country club · huntington quadrangle · imrex computers · infiniti of greenwich · ipark · irving tire · island sports · jablow · jacob · jacobson · jaeger · jaffe · janowitz · japan airlines · jassey medical facility · jeffer · jena hall · jericel · jfwb interiors · jobco · jones · justin · k&f building · kadden · kadish · kahn · kalikow · kalnick · kaltman · kandel · kaneff · kantor · kaplan · kase · katime · katz · kauff · kavazis · kensington school · kent · kesten · kimmel · king kullen · kings point village hall · klee · klein · klockner · koenigsberg · koeppel · kolin industrial · koroseal showroom · kossoy · kotsonis · kra · kramer · krasner · kremer · krieg consulting · krim · krons chocolate · krosser · krug · krypell · kurzrok · la fitness · labelle · laccone · lake grove shopping center · lally · lamle · landau · landmark capital · landmark stationers · lane · lang · lasdon · latman · lazare · lebowitz · lee · lefrak · leigh · lenowitz · leonards · leventhal · levy · lexel corporation · lieber · lifetree technologies · liguori · lij hospital · lilco · lilker associates · limmer · lincoln stationers · linotype · lipshutz · loeb · london · looking glass · lostritto · luccarelli offices · luxenberg · mack · mahendru ·

DEDICATION

'To my children, you inspire me to continue to build a modern world for
your future.'   -Tom

'To my dad, thank you for inspiring me to discover my strengths through
all your hard work and talent. To my wife, Susan, and my children, Ylana,
Scott, and Allison, for their total support and inspiration through the years;
all the laughs and memories have kept me together.'   -Mark

MOJO · STUMER ASSOCIATES

Library of Congress Cataloging in Publication Data:
Design Excellence

ISBN 13: 978-0-9825989-1-7
ISBN 10: 0-9825989-1-2

Distributors to the trade in the United States and Canada
Innovative Logistics
575 Prospect Street
Lakewood, NJ 08701
732.363.5679

Distributors outside the United States and Canada
HarperCollins International
10 East 53rd Street
New York, NY 10022-5299

Exclusive distributor in China
Beijing Designerbooks Co., Ltd.
B-0619, No.2 Building, Dacheng International Center
78 East 4th Ring Middle Road
Chaoyang District, Beijing 100022, P.R. China
Tel: 0086(010)5962-6195 Fax: 0086(010)5962-6193
E-mail: info@designerbooks.net   www.designerbooks.net

Book Design: Veronika Levin & Martina Parisi
Design Editors: Michael Spitaleri & Katina Max Kremelberg
Editorial Directors: Roger Yee, Colby Brock, and
Katina Max Kremelberg
Printed and bound in China
The paper on which this book is printed contains
recycled content to support a sustainable world.

DESIGN EXCELLENCE

VISUAL PROFILE BOOKS, INC., NEW YORK

TABLE OF CONTENTS

FOREWORD

I met Mark Stumer when I was 20 years old. Full of rampant energy and creative charisma, Mark instantly commanded my attention. I intently listened in on a meeting he was having with a client that he had worked with for years; my father, Peter Brock. The project we were about to embark on was a renovation of a hotel in New York. I was a novice in the design industry, my curiosity only peeked by Mark's passion. After thoroughly discussing the depths of his concept for this job, the two men bantered back and forth about the first time they worked together. "Tom and I had just started to put Mojo Stumer together. Peter called me and asked me to meet him at the site for his new project, a restaurant, Cartoons, on the South Shore of Long Island. It was 1978. Wow, we were young." They chuckled; I marveled. Fortunately, after working with Mark on that hotel project and developing a close friendship, I decided to turn my professional attention to interior design. Since then, I have been working side by side with my mentor, Mark, as well as Tom Mojo and the team that trademarked MSA as an architectural & interior design powerhouse. Before owning their own label of modern architecture, Mark and Tom came from modest origins; each enticed by architecture at a young age.

Mark was born an architect, pulling Frank Lloyd Wright books off library shelves at 6 years old. He followed closely in the footsteps of generations of men in his family; his great grandfather, grandfather and father. They all used their hands to help craft the concrete foundations of New York. But Mark set his sights on conducting the construction orchestra by becoming an architect. Tom Mojo's beginnings were not a far departure from that of his partner. "It began with my father always shouting at me 'you can't talk without a pen in your hand, son'. He was right and to this day, that remains true." Tom found himself in Saint Mark's Square in 1963, while enlisted in the United States Navy. In that moment he felt in his heart that he had found what he was meant to do. He was drawn to the idea of contributing to architectural history and knew that one day he would.

Indeed, Mojo Stumer Associates has risen from its inception to be one of the most respected names in modern architecture and design. After thirty years of working together, Mark and Tom have perfected their architectural waltz; each step synchronized to the beat of their modern masterpieces, perfectly juxtaposed ideas and concepts, working in harmony to create commercial and residential projects that all bear their unique signature. The MSA philosophy is the synergy of exterior edifices and interior spaces giving rise to a complete purpose. Whether you want to view their body of work as a whole, or as statements of their individuality, the transformation of what begins as a moved sketch to the contemporary structures of glass, steel and stone that line the landscapes of New York, Florida and other parts of the world, are certainly those of a team that has written a chapter in 21st century architecture.

The establishment of Mojo Stumer Associates, p.c. happened in 1980 after Mark and Tom left another New York firm together to explore their own architectural ambitions. With their learned business practices, in conjunction with the ideologies of their architectural muses, they decidedly cultivated a firm that focuses on personal relationships both with clients and colleagues. You can look to the hundreds of clients that live and work in Mojo Stumer designs to see that there is a certain love affair that they have with their surroundings. The architecture, both commercial and residential, speaks to them; their needs; their desires, the sheer satisfaction of knowing that what was created for them is uniquely theirs. It's sublime. Mark & Tom are able to reflect their modern instincts and transition, what is typically referred to as a style that is "unlivable," into an ingratiating, timeless space. This talent has catapulted them into the success that they continue to work for everyday.

The pair has shared the same objectives since they began this journey. Everything they do is related to the design they love. They do not run their firm as an enterprise, rather, as inspired artists; 95% architects and 5% business men. Sometimes to a fault, however, there is no such thing as sacrificing their architectural integrity, regardless of profit and loss statements. The belief they hold so strongly to is that there will always be another opportunity to add to the bottom line, but not another opportunity to do the very best we can in the moment we are living in now. At the end of the day, architects create a lifestyle and each project leaves a lasting impression of who that architect is and what signature they hope to leave behind.

In retrospect, Mojo and Stumer recall all the significant relationships they have forged in the past thirty years, many of which influenced them and remain strong to this day. In particular, they remember a series of introductions to some of New York's pioneer developers, namely Jack Wexler, Jack Goodstein, Gilbert Tilles, Robert Kaufman, Morris Saznauer and Burt Mack and his family, marked points in the duo's career, asserting that they had reached a particular level of success. Yet, the person who inspires them most is the late Charles Gwathmey. A true modernist architect, never wavering from his patented style, whose work monumentally shaped the 21st century. Just as their icon, they have empowered their work to represent them and what they love most, modern architecture. To know them, is to know what they have built.

From humble beginnings to the legacy that they have only begun to build, the team of Mojo Stumer, along with their dedicated associates, projects managers, project architects, interior designers & interns, has certainly risen to the stature that the team set their sights on some thirty years ago.

-Colby Brock

INTRODUCTION

We at Mojo-Stumer Associates, MSA, practice architecture, and interior design, because we love it. We have never wanted to do anything else with our lives. Architecture is not our profession, it is our religion. Our passion and experience has brought us to a pinnacle moment in our 30 year history. As a new chapter begins for us, we'd like to celebrate what has brought us here; as a firm, a team and a family.

Our past has taught us to appreciate adding to the field of architecture and separating ourselves from the masses. We accomplish that by thriving on unexpected juxtapositions; modern exteriors defined by bold planes, complemented by contemporary interiors that are exceptionally livable. Our work is not just for viewing. It's meant to be experienced personally. This premise has led to our design mission-improving the quality of our clients' lives through better and more creative architecture and interior design.

Put aside your predispositions towards modern architecture and look at our work with fresh eyes. Many people still do not understand modernism nearly a century after its debut. More often than not, they tend to believe the style is incapable of being warm and inviting. Our hope is that you regard our buildings with a sense of wonder, slightly confounded that your preconceived notions were amiss, but joyful that modern architecture can be so much more than what you thought it would be.

South Palm Beach Apartment

Palm Beach, FL

Kings Point Waterfront Home

Kings Point, NY

Bank of Smithtown

Huntington, NY

HISTORY

Mojo-Stumer Associates was founded in 1980 by two friends, and colleagues, who wanted to challenge the constraints of the built world. Thomas J. Mojo, AIA, and Mark D.Stumer, AIA, intended to do nothing less than create a brand of architecture that spoke to the modern world in which we live. MSA was born with the intention of exposing contemporary designs' virtually unlimited breadth and depth.

Our mission has been uncommonly successful. We received our first award from the American Institute of Architects in 1982 and our first magazine cover was published by Interior Design in 1991. Since our inception, MSA has won repeated recognition for its achievements.

The past 30 years have given us invaluable insight. By engaging clients and communities in everyday situations, we turn goals and visions into effective physical realities. Design evolves incrementally, and our work only improves with experience. We are more capable of understanding and anticipating environmental, personal, and organizational challenges today than we did yesterday.

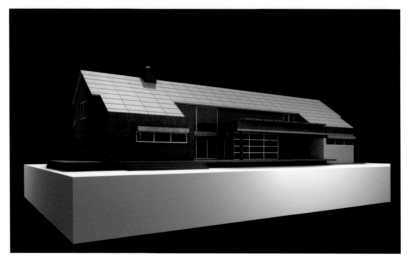

Hewlett Packard

Melville, NY

Dune Road Retreat

East Quogue, NY

Salem Country Estate

North Salem, NY

South Beach Apartment

Miami, FL

Palm Beach Residence

Palm Beach, FL

PHILOSOPHY

Through the creative process we are able to express our individuality. The team of Mojo-Stumer Associates, MSA, is able to realize our own ambitions as well as those of our clients by trusting in this process. By encouraging the development of creativity in our clients, we help society to live outside the standardized box of strip malls and fast food chains.

What goes into each project is as unique as the hopes, circumstances, resources and challenges it encompasses. What remains consistent throughout, however, is our methodology. Our design process is a far cry from whimsical. Rather, it is predicated on the development of ideas that will ensure the most successful outcome. MSA works with our clients through their projects, making the progression easy and the results always make us proud. Over the years we have formulated our own system for nurturing architecture from concept to reality. We firmly believe in strict programming and analysis. The synthesis of design philosophy, program requirements and site needs are an integral part of our methodology. All these components of project development allow us to execute a schematic design solution that responds faithfully to our clients' concerns. We pride ourselves on our deductive approach because it positively sets our finished products apart from other firms.

Our clients are sophisticated and understand the value of exceptional architecture. They seek to enhance their lifestyle and express originality through design. Our clients undoubtedly know and expect great work from us.

Temple Young Israel

Great Neck, NY

Equinox

New York, NY

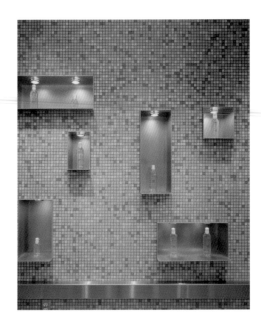

Washington DC Penthouse

Washington, DC

COMMERCIAL

Business people wonder why they should care about architecture. We can demonstrate that good design yields multiple benefits for our commercial and corporate clients. You can achieve a more efficient work environment through carefully considered design, which also vests your company with an image of success and reputability. Moreover, your employees will respect the safety, security and comfort of a well-designed workplace.

While the blueprint of an office is ideally tailored to the organization that occupies it, the typical business approach is simple. Many office building tenants customarily follow the fit out advice of the landlord to keep costs down. There are some situations in which this is inconsequential and will favor the business owner. MSA strives to create commercial designs that will foster businesses that want to provide professional services and wish to be perceived as superior to competitors. Through our experience, we have gained an invaluable understanding of the internal structure of a business. This insight allows us to predict what a company will need architecturally to nurture its growth.

Providing enhanced visual, acoustical and thermal comfort helps to motivate a highly productive staff. Shoppers tend to flock towards more aesthetically pleasing retail spaces, and are likely to spend more time and money in a well-designed shopping environment. In today's increasingly visual world, a successful workplace design is becoming the hallmark of a successful business.

Prentice Capital

New York, NY

Long Island Boat House

Kings Point, NY

GB Capital

New York, NY

MSA Offices

Greenvale, NY

Midtown Apartment

New York, NY

Cline Davis Mann Conference Room

New York, NY

RESIDENTIAL

Our contemporary homes compliment the lifestyle of our clients and shelter a comfortable way of living. Formal, austere and minimally detailed residences may have prevailed at the dawn of the modern era. However, with the advance of contemporary residential style, there has been a dramatic turn towards materials, finishes and furnishings that render modern design highly livable, so "modern living" is no longer an oxymoron. Today's dwelling is a radical departure from past notions that unless a home is traditional in style, it cannot be traditional in spirit. With all the stressful situations the modern family must face, it deserves to find sanctuary—along with timeless comfort, convenience and beauty—in a modern home.

Each home we design is a joint creation between architect and client. That is essential to the way we work. We are avid proponents of the "dream" you entrust to us. It helps to set us on our course in the beginning of each project. The more you push us with your initial vision, the more we push ourselves to be inventive and try new techniques. It's safe to say there is never one expert with all the answers when you're translating ideas into reality.Outstanding homes are the products of talented artists and discerning families working together to find solutions.

Since we demand more from ourselves than clients expect, they should prepare to be surprised and delighted. We strive to exceed their hopes and create flawless, innovative architecture and interior design for each project. We find our greatest elation when clients are fulfilled by the work we do.

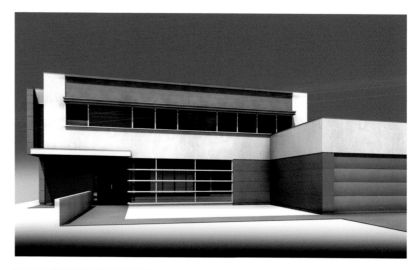

East Side Penthouse
New York, NY

Florida Residence

Palm Beach, FL

Barley Ziecheck Medical Offices

New York, NY

INTERIORS

MSA regards architecture and interior design as cohesive elements of one holistic built environment; inseparable, as a tree from its roots. We welcome each opportunity to juxtapose a building's program, adjacencies and circulation with furniture, material, and environment. We use interiors to enhance our projects, turning our architecture into a canvas for our interior design.

Clients sometimes question what benefits come from using a professional interior designer: simply, experience, imagination and expertise. Our projects consistently result in interiors of outstanding comfort, beauty and luxury. With each job, we learn how to do things more efficiently—in terms of time, cost and technique—to the advantage of our clients. To create a unique interior that speaks to and about one's personality, there is no substitute for an interior designer.

Often the exterior and interior of a building seem surprisingly unrelated. Although the effect can be stifling, the situation is easily remedied. Architecture evokes a certain feeling, with respect to scale and proportion, of exterior elements. It is along these same lines that we carry our design to the interiors, instilling a sense of comfort as one moves through our spaces. Our interiors always have a dialogue and a connection with our exteriors, ensuring the end result is always a cohesive whole. Yet, the elements still maintain architectural individuality onto themselves.

Old Westbury Residence

Old Westbury, NY

Park Avenue Home

New York, NY

Miami Beach Apartment

Miami, FL

Nubest

Manhasset, NY

HOSPITALITY

Hospitality industry employees, whether in a hotel, country club, exercise facility, restaurant or bar, are quite literally on stage for their customers. Indeed, hotel guests and restaurant patrons expect a "show" in public spaces. It's not by accident that the hospitality industry and show business share terms such as "back of house," "front of house," "it's show time," and "you're on." Whenever we design hospitality facilities, we at MSA have to pay attention to what happens in the front of the house, where the customers watch the show, and the back of house, where the employees must complete the tasks that help the show go on.

Smooth operations are essential to the hospitality business. The back of the house ensures staff productivity, conceals employee tasks from customers, supports flow and circulation throughout front of house, and houses all of the equipment necessary to run the business. Therefore, we take the time to make sure back of house spaces function as effectively as their front of house counterparts.

Good hospitality design not only draws customers in, it inspires them to share their experience with others. We focus primarily on providing comfort for the guests in a distinctive setting. Combined with great service, our design ensures a memorable occasion that entices people to frequent our client's establishments—and generates the priceless word-of-mouth referrals that attract more customers.

Boca Rio Country Club

Boca Raton, FL

Boca Raton Residence

Boca Raton, FL

New York City Apartment

New York, NY

I-Park Complex

Lake Success, NY

Related Companies

New York, NY

Lorraine Boutique

Great Neck, NY

New City Residence

New City, NY

East River Apartment

New York, NY

AWARDS

From the start, our firm has sought to illuminate the mind's eye by pushing the limits of what is possible in architecture and interior design. MSA shows leadership in our profession by continuing to seek intrinsic value in international competition. We consider every design award we receive as a symbol of success in our quest.

Besides indicating that our work is respected among our peers, awards reaffirm that our clients value our work. Our success is their success. Winning recognition within our field allows our clients to share in the history of our firm.

We have been fortunate to receive many significant awards during our first 30 years. To name a few: The *AIA's Young Firm Award, AIA Design Awards, Archi Awards, IBD Awards, Ceramic Tile Awards, Benjamin Moore Awards, Subzero Awards* and *Interiors Magazine National Awards*. We retain the ability to surprise and awe, marking a tradition that we continue to pursue.

We're Group

Jericho, NY

Watermill Residence

Watermill, NY

Upper West Side Apartment

New York, NY

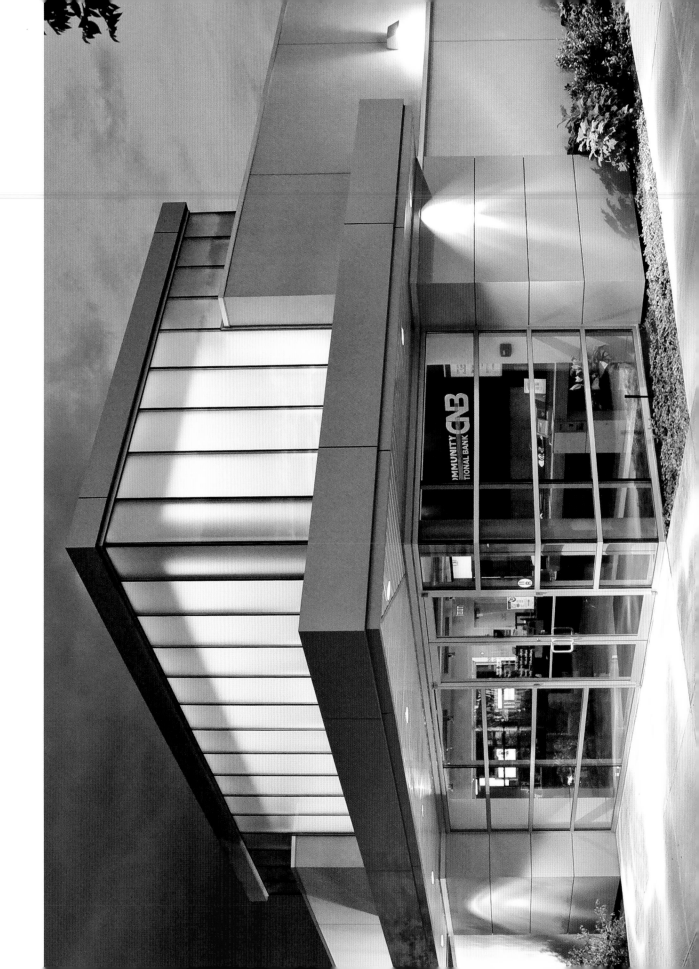

Community National Bank

Woodbury, NY and New Hyde Park, NY

LOOKING AHEAD

We promise our clients, colleagues and friends that we will maintain the tradition of Design Excellence that we have steadily cultivated during the past three decades. We are determined to keep finding ingenious ways to improve upon the built world in which we live. We will strive to be better every day.

We will incorporate new methods and materials into our repertoire and look forward to the new clients and projects in years to come. By embracing our existing practices and implementing promising new ideas, MSA will keep evolving. So much of what we love is adding to our environment, not taking away from it. Hence, the practice of sustainable design allows us to continue lining landscapes and sprinkling skylines with punctuated architecture for future generations.

The late Charles Gwathmey once said, "we wanted to prove that architecture was not only about image, but about idea," (associates press, 2010). In the pursuit of continuing to shape those ideas about modern architecture, we will remain in the struggle to redefine what modern is for our clients and for the world, proving Mr. Gwathmey's dogma ever true.

Realm

New York, NY

Great Neck Home

Great Neck Estates, NY

Tribeca Triplex

New York, NY

Private Yacht Interiors

Past Employees

Diego Aguilera
Guirleen Anderson
Jasmine Bacchus
Elsye Barbara
Diane Bialo
Nicole Blankfeld
Reina Bronz
Jackie Brown
Maximo Buschfrer
Diane Chizzoniti
Leo Cordoba
James Cowan
Ben Cruz
Mark Dekenipp
J. Depalma
Daniel Dicapite
Susan Disalvo
Eduardo Dunphy
Toni Anne Ekberg
Christopher Eng
Andrew Etter
Daniel Fabrizi
Susan Faulhaber
Karen Fisher
Robert Fleming
Michael Fokianois
Joseph Franchina
Tiffany Gavin
Joseph Giovaniello
N. Goldberg
Iesha Gomillion
Michael Graziosi
Ian Greenberg
Sandra Hayman
Shashime Haywood
Irene Ioffe
Jennifer Johnson
Wendi Johnson
Sophia Kahn
Peter Kladias
Demetra Koulizakis
Elena Lechinsky
Heide Lihme
Jessica Lopipero

Rupert Maddock
Charlene Marstiller
Suzanne Mazzara
David McGullam
Terrance McKeen
William Minnear
Jeffrey Mongno
Albert Monsanto
Robert Montefusco
Sharon Moore
Thomas Murawski
Todd Patane
Ashish Patel
Burcu Permuz
Enrique Pincay
Maria Pirraglia
Justin Pogrob
Anthony Polito
Melissa Pollack
Jose Reyes
Ellen Roche
Diana Rook
Javier Salinas
Rachel Salvatore
Denise Sauer
Ana Serra
Walter Smith
Maria Sola
Rachel Stone
M. Sudano
Jaclyn Sumer
Emilio Susa
Imre Szabo
Thomas Tait
Sergio Tedesco
Betsy Varughese
Natalie Vicari
Renate Walker
Marcus Williams
Robert Williams
Beata Wroblewski
Andrew Wynnyk
Casey Yui
Michael Zampini
J. Zanotti

Interns

Bari Abrams
Harriet Andronikides
Enis Baskahya
Ryan Cataldi
Indraneel Dutta
Adam Feit
Dari Horowitz
Herby Joseph
Sasha Kaufman
Claire Kim
Stephanie Marotta
Jessica Migden
Jigar Patel
Mowdood Popal
Anne Marie Porcaro
Prachoom Reck
Jessica Samaroo
Eric Smith
Chris Stoddard
Ylana Stumer
Ever Umana

STAFF

Principals

Thomas Mojo
Mark Stumer

Colby Brock
JoAnn Burgreen
Peter Cho
Patricia Dougherty
Michael Doyle
Lisa Gross
Catherine Hurwitz
Peter Johns
Katina Max Kremelberg
Jessica Licalzi
Lance McAllister
Roberto Miatello
Kimberly Mohan
Trevor Morris
Richard Rosa
Michael Spitaleri
Sharlene Teitel
Charles Wolf
Jack Zuccon

malco consulting · malekan · mall center · managistics · manetto hills · manhasset bay yacht club · manhasset mammography · manhattan motors · marcus · marine midland bank · marino · marowitz · marquez · mascioli · mason hotel · masone shopping center · massapequa general hospital · massapequa shops · maurer · mayer · mazzoni · mccance · mcdonald · mchugh · meadow springs · meenan oil · meltzer · memmi · merberg · meringoff · meshel · messados · metro fuel · metsch · meyers · micles shoe corporation · mill river club · millbrook apartments · miller · mineola shopping center · miner · mitchell field · mittasch · monahan · mondowin mall · montauk shoppes · monti · morel · morse · moskowitz · moss · motschwiller · mount sinai senior center · munsey park retail shoppes · muttontown country club · myerson · nadler · nassau county medical center · nassau county museum of art · nassau-suffolk council · nasser · national guild for the blind · naughton · neely · neil auto dealerships · nemeroff · nevans · new rochelle mri · newman · nicholson · north hempstead country club · north hills country club · north shore country club · north shore university hospital · northridge · nubest · nussdorf · nycom · o'grady · oakdale cinema · odette · old mill inn · olsten · oltchick · olympus · omni mri · operative cake · oppenheim · orion · orlin · ornstein · osipow · ostad · pace · paley · palin · paolino · parker medical · parker waichman · parlante · parr · patent · paul anthony aesthetics · pelham bay medical · penn · penn auto dealerships · pergament · perlmutter · pete's golf shop · petracca · philips offices · phoenix hotel · pierucci · pine hollow country club · podell · polikoff · polimeni offices · pollack · polo club · portokai · posner · postal · prentice capital · primi · production packaging · proman · prudent auto dealerships · puglisi · pullo · pullo metro fuel · pure · puton · quality auto · rabin · rabiner · radbell · radisson hotel · rakosi · raphael · raskin · ravner · realm · rechler · reckson associates · reh marketing · related offices · rfi corporation · rich · richards · ripka · riverbay · rivers gift shop · robins · rockmore · rockville center mri · rockville jewish center · roestenberg · rogoff · rogove · rohrlich · romanelli · rose · rosen · ross · roth · rothberg · rothstein · roti · rotter · rousso · rubell · rubenstein · rubies costume company · rubins · rubinstein · rudco industries · rudnick · rudolph · russo · sahn · saint kilian parish · sakosits · salm · san marzano restaurant · sanders · sandler · sanford · santolli · sasso · satten · sayville · scharf · scheffler · scheiner · schiavone · schiffman · schlanger · schlossberg · schmergel · schneider · schoenfeld · school for language · schulman realty · schultz · schur · schwartz · schweber · sculpture associates · sealove · sebag · segal consulting · seiden · seidenfeld · seifer · senter · serbin · sergi · servo · shamosh · shapiro · shari's place · sherman · sherwyn · shogren · shonfeld · shulman · siegel · silverman · silverstein · singer · sitomer · ski · skolnick · skurnik wines · slaine · sleepy's corporate headquarters · smart money 500 · smith · sohn · soltz · somar interiors · something physical · sonometrics · sorkin · south plainfeld · south shore fitness · south shore gastroenterology · spark creation · sparks · sperling · spielman · spivak · sportime · stanford athletic club · state farm · station plaza · steel-los · stein · sterling · steuben foods · steven corn furs · stiepleman insurance · stone · success medical · sullivan mri · sunrise day camp · superior packaging · sutherland · swan club · swift · taubmann office complex · teitler · tellabs · temple beth el · temple young israel · terminal drive · the colorado · the fur vault · the halo group · the nines · the we're group · third dimensions · thor development · thypin steel · travelers insurance · trinity church · tristate · tritec · turquie · usher · v.j. associates · vahradian · valle · vanbergen · vert · virtual reality · vitco · wachtlar law offices · wagman · wain · waksal · waldners · walton · wand · wang · wax · weber offices · webster bank · weeks lerman · weinberg · weinberg · weingrow · weiss · weitz · wernick · westhampton bath & tennis · wexler · wheatley hills golf club · white · wincom · winston · winston plaza · wired environments · wisser · wk equities · wolf insurance · wolokoff · wolosoff · woodbury salon · woodcrest country club · woodmere country club · wurtzburg · wyckoff · yasgur · young · young woo · zanghi development · zarin · zeccardi · zeluck · zetlin · zicherman · zigelbaum · zimmerman · zucker · 1-800-Flowers · 21st century marketing